GROUNDWOOD BOOKS
HOUSE OF ANANSI PRESS
TORONTO   BERKELEY

And So It Goes

by Paloma Valdivia

Translated by
Susan Ouriou

First published in Spanish as *Es así* by Paloma Valdivia
Copyright © 2010 by Fondo de Cultura Económica
Carretera Picacho Ajusco 227, C.P. 14378, México, D.F.
English translation copyright © 2017 by Susan Ouriou
First published in English in Canada and the USA in 2017
by Groundwood Books

Groundwood Books / House of Anansi Press
groundwoodbooks.com

We acknowledge the Government of Canada for its financial support of our
publishing program.

With the participation of the Government of Canada
Avec la participation du gouvernement du Canada | Canadä

Library and Archives Canada Cataloguing in Publication
Valdivia, Paloma
[Es asi. English]
And so it goes / Paloma Valdivia ; translated by Susan Ouriou.
Translation of: Es así.
Issued in print and electronic formats.
ISBN 978-1-55498-869-3 (hardcover). — ISBN 978-1-55498-870-9 (PDF)
 I. Ouriou, Susan, translator II. Title. III. Title: Es asi. English.
PZ7.V253Es 2017   j863'.7   C2016-908228-8
C2016-908229-6

The illustrations were done in watercolor, pencil, ink and Photoshop.
Printed and bound in Malaysia

For Guillem, who'll arrive
one fine spring day.
We are preparing a party
for him.

Some have already left.

The neighbor's cat, Aunt Margarita,
the fish in yesterday's soup.

Others will arrive.
Some were longed for,
others come out of the blue.

Those of us here
weep tears for those who leave.

It feels good
to remember them

Those of us here
rejoice over those who arrive.
We make them welcome —
we love to celebrate.

For a fleeting moment, those who leave and those who arrive cross paths in the air.

They wish each other happiness.

Those who leave don't know where they're going.

Their destination doesn't depend on the wind or how old they are.

La Lupita

Those who arrive don't know either.
Life's just like that, it seems — up to chance.

It's a mystery where they come from
and where they're headed.

Those of us here are just here.
And so we'd best enjoy ourselves.

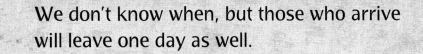

We don't know when, but those who arrive
will leave one day as well.

And so it goes,
just as spring follows winter.
Some arrive while others
take their leave.